ultimate
DOT TO DOT
ANIMALS

Extreme puzzle challenges
to complete and color

PUZZLES BY DR. GARETH MOORE

B.Sc. (Hons) M.Phil., Ph.D.

T0025909

Connect the dots to reveal the amazing animal pictures in this book. There are 30 puzzles for you to complete and color. Each page can be pulled out and displayed when you have finished.

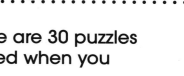

Instructions:

- Start at number 1, marked with a hollow star, and then draw lines to each numbered dot until you reach a hollow dot.

- When you reach a hollow dot, take your pen off the page and move to the next number, which will also have a hollow dot. Then, continue drawing lines from dot to dot.

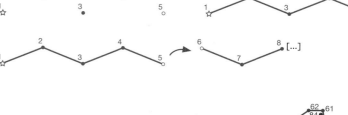

- The dots and associated numbers are colored, indicating the color recommended to use for the line through those dots.

- The final dot on each puzzle is also marked with a hollow star.

Hints & Tips:

- If you aren't immediately sure which dot is attached to each number, look at the surrounding dots and numbers to work it out.

- Use a fine-tipped pen or pencil so that you don't obscure dots and numbers you haven't yet used.

- You don't have to start at number 1—you can start anywhere you like and then fill in the parts you've missed later.

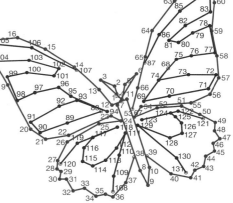

- Don't worry if you make a mistake—it's very unlikely that you'll be able to notice it once you have completed the final image, thanks to the intricate nature of each of the pictures.

- You don't have to use the suggested colors if you don't want to—feel free to pick your own.

- Once you have joined all of the dots, you can color in the picture with pens or pencils.

- There is a small, finished version of each image at the back of the book.

- Visit *www.mombooks.com/activities* to see larger solutions for each puzzle.

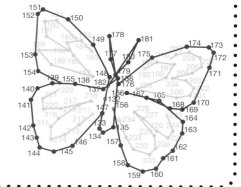

sourcebooks

Copyright © 2017, 2022 by Michael O'Mara Books
Puzzle copyright © 2017 by Dr. Gareth Moore

Sourcebooks and the colophon are registered trademarks of Sourcebooks.

All rights reserved. No part of this book may be reproduced in any form or by any electronic or mechanical means including information storage and retrieval systems—except in the case of brief quotations

embodied in critical articles or reviews—without permission in writing from its publisher, Sourcebooks.

This publication is designed to provide accurate and authoritative information in regard to the subject matter covered. It is sold with the understanding that the publisher is not engaged in rendering legal, accounting, or other professional service. If legal advice or other expert assistance is required, the services of a competent professional person should be sought.

—From a Declaration of Principles Jointly Adopted by a Committee of the American Bar Association and a Committee of Publishers and Associations

Published by Sourcebooks
P.O. Box 4410, Naperville, Illinois 60567-4410
(630) 961-3900 • sourcebooks.com

First published in Great Britain in 2017 by Michael O'Mara Books Limited. This edition issued based on the

paperback edition published in 2017 in North America by B.E.S. Publishing.

Library of Congress Cataloging-in-Publication Data is on file with the publisher.

Printed and bound in China.
OGP 10 9 8 7 6 5 4 3 2

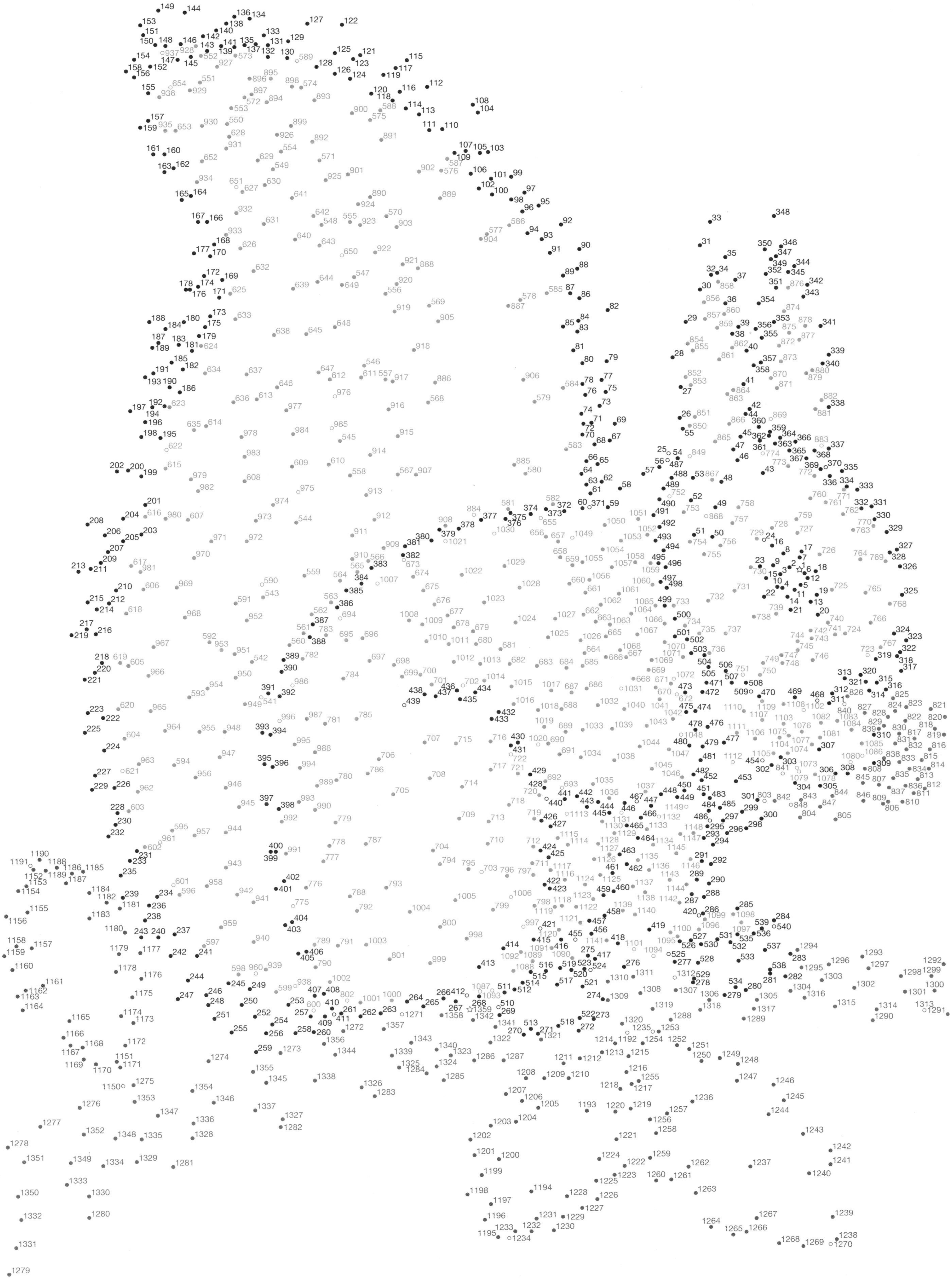

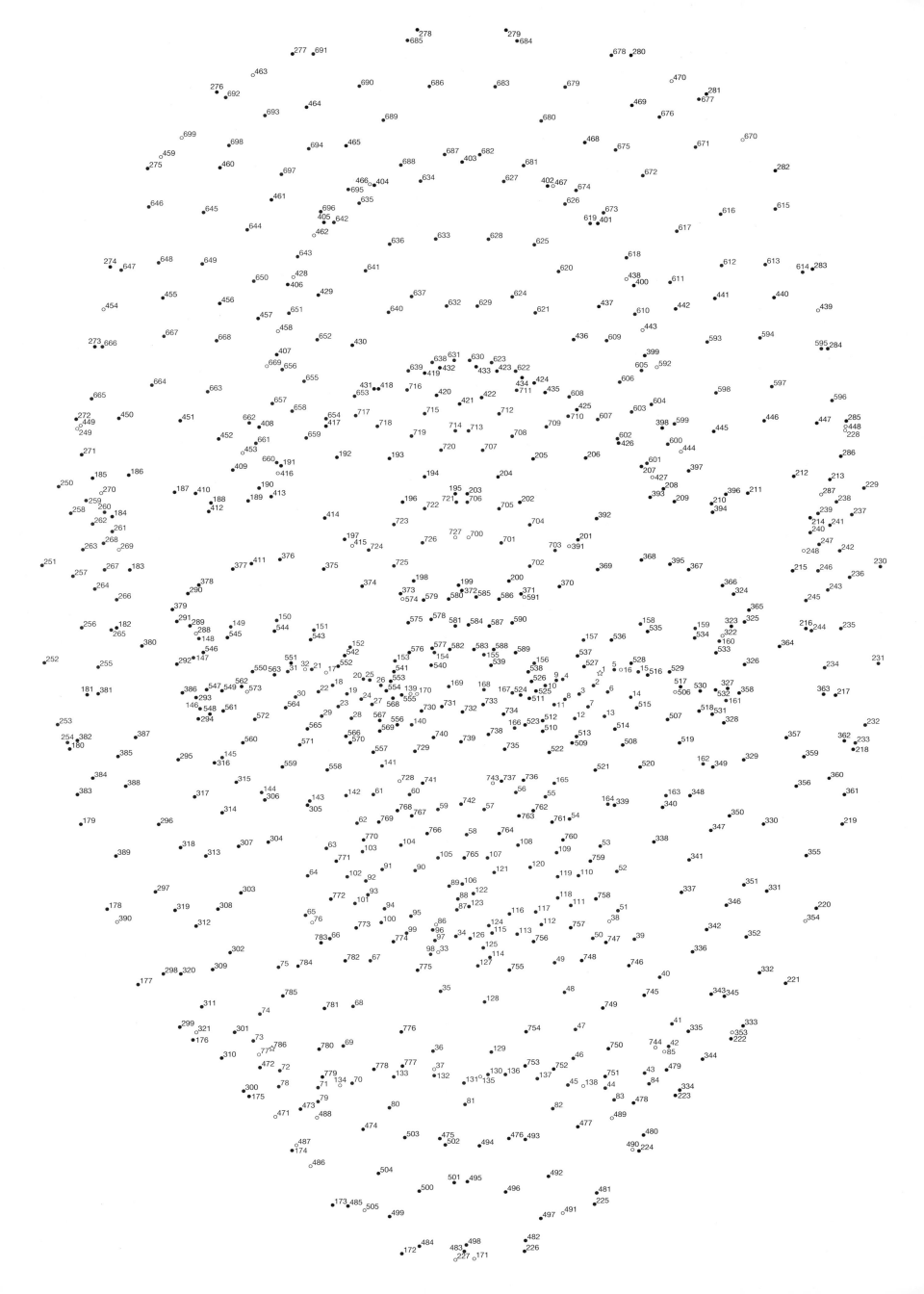

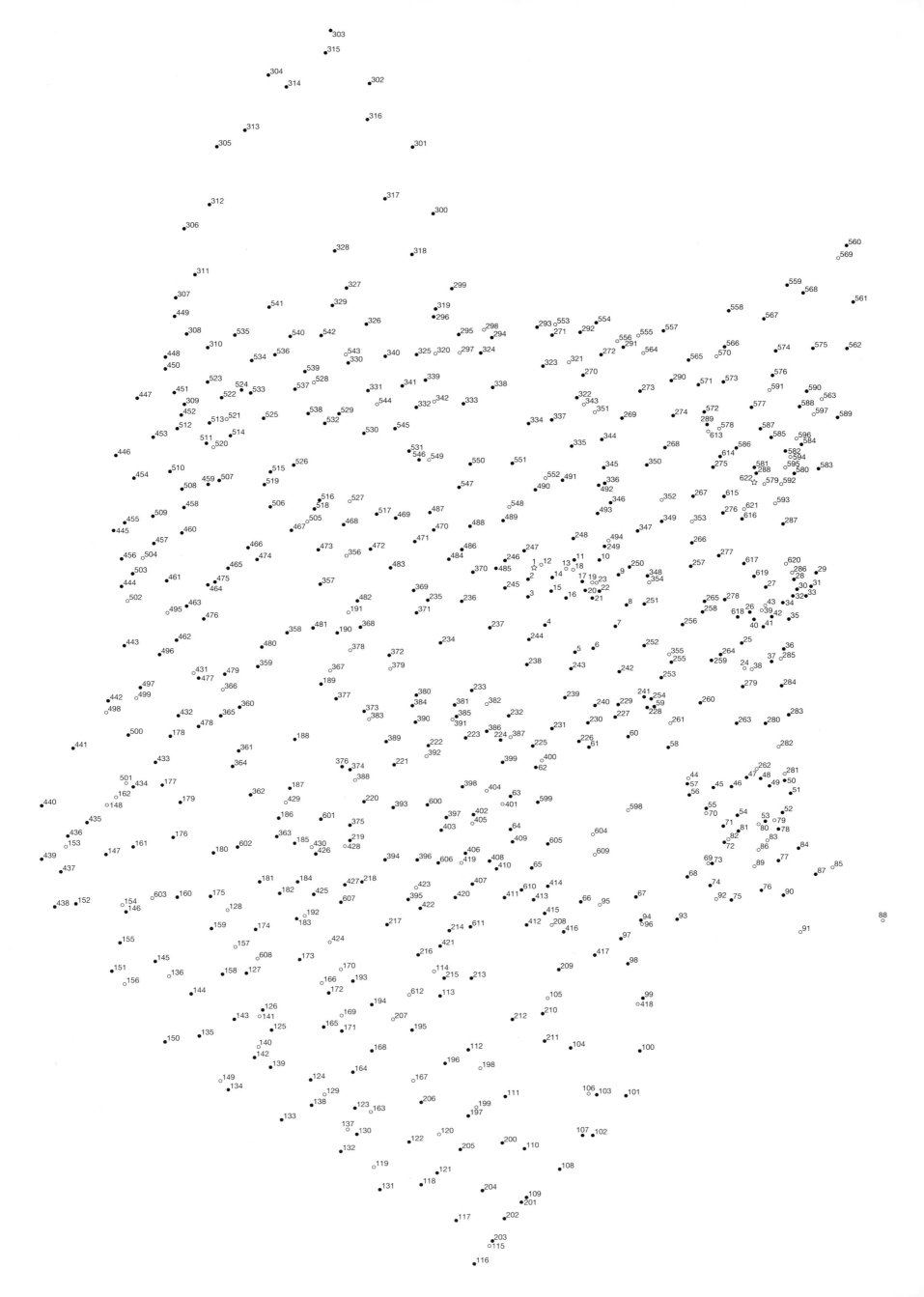

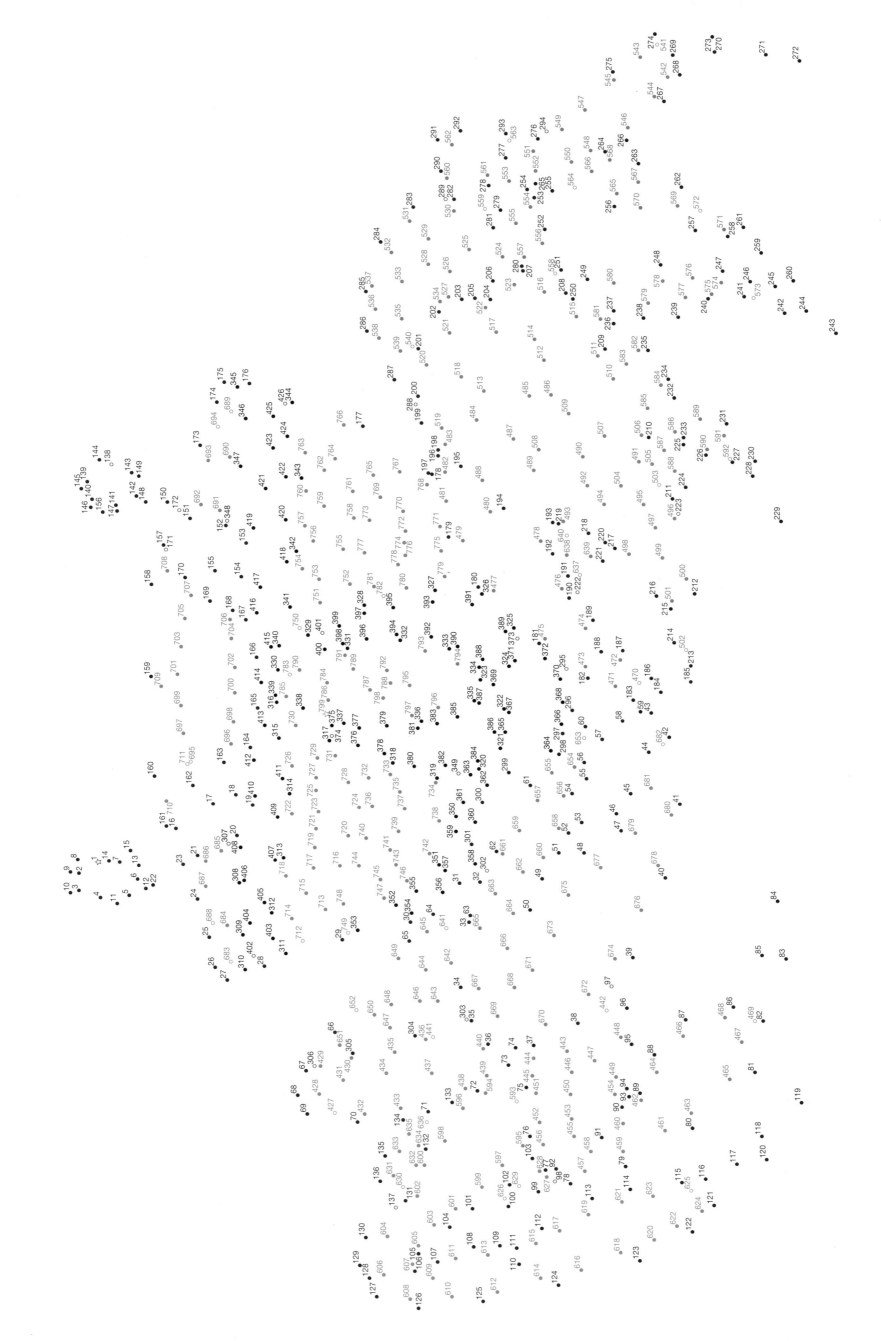

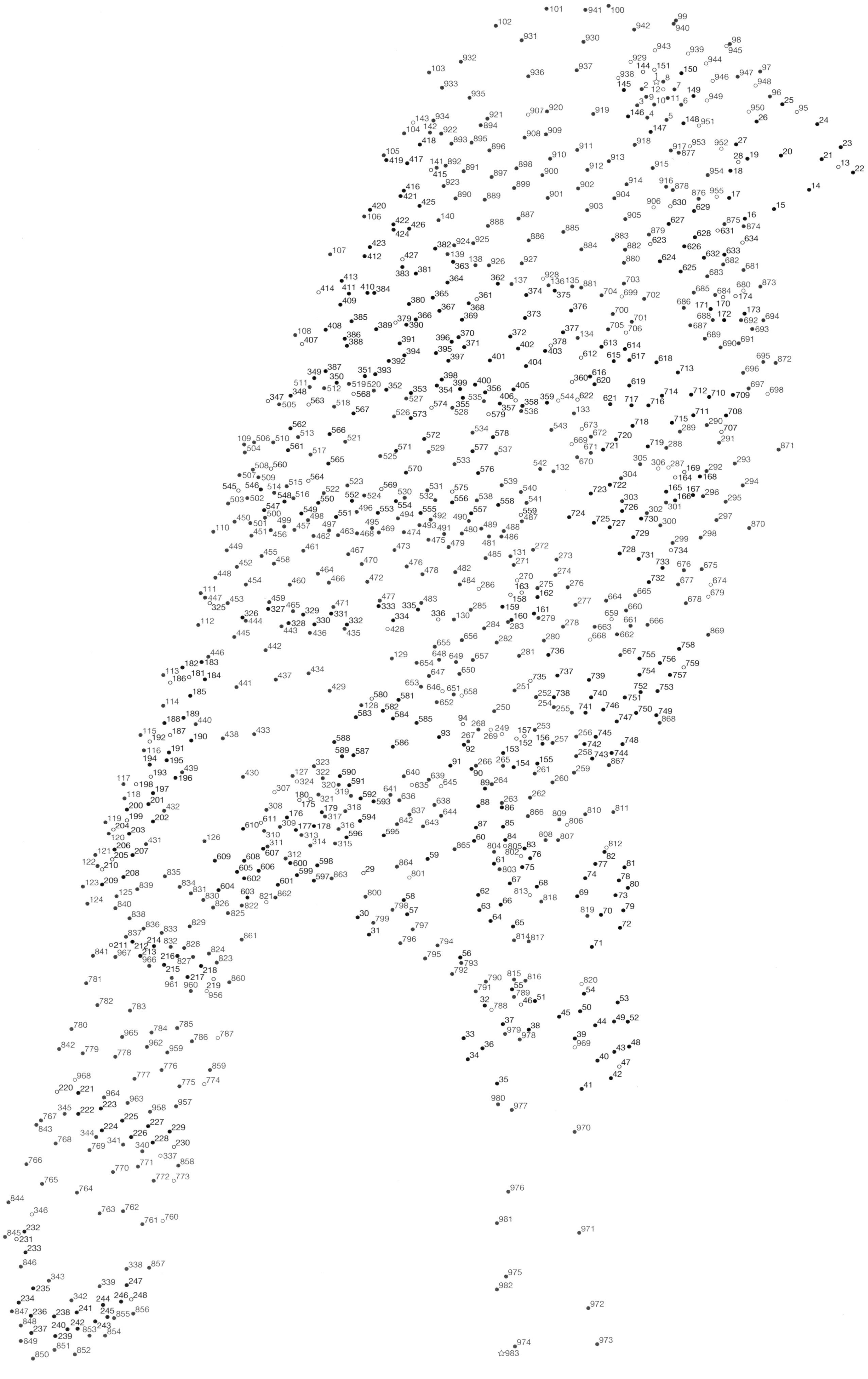

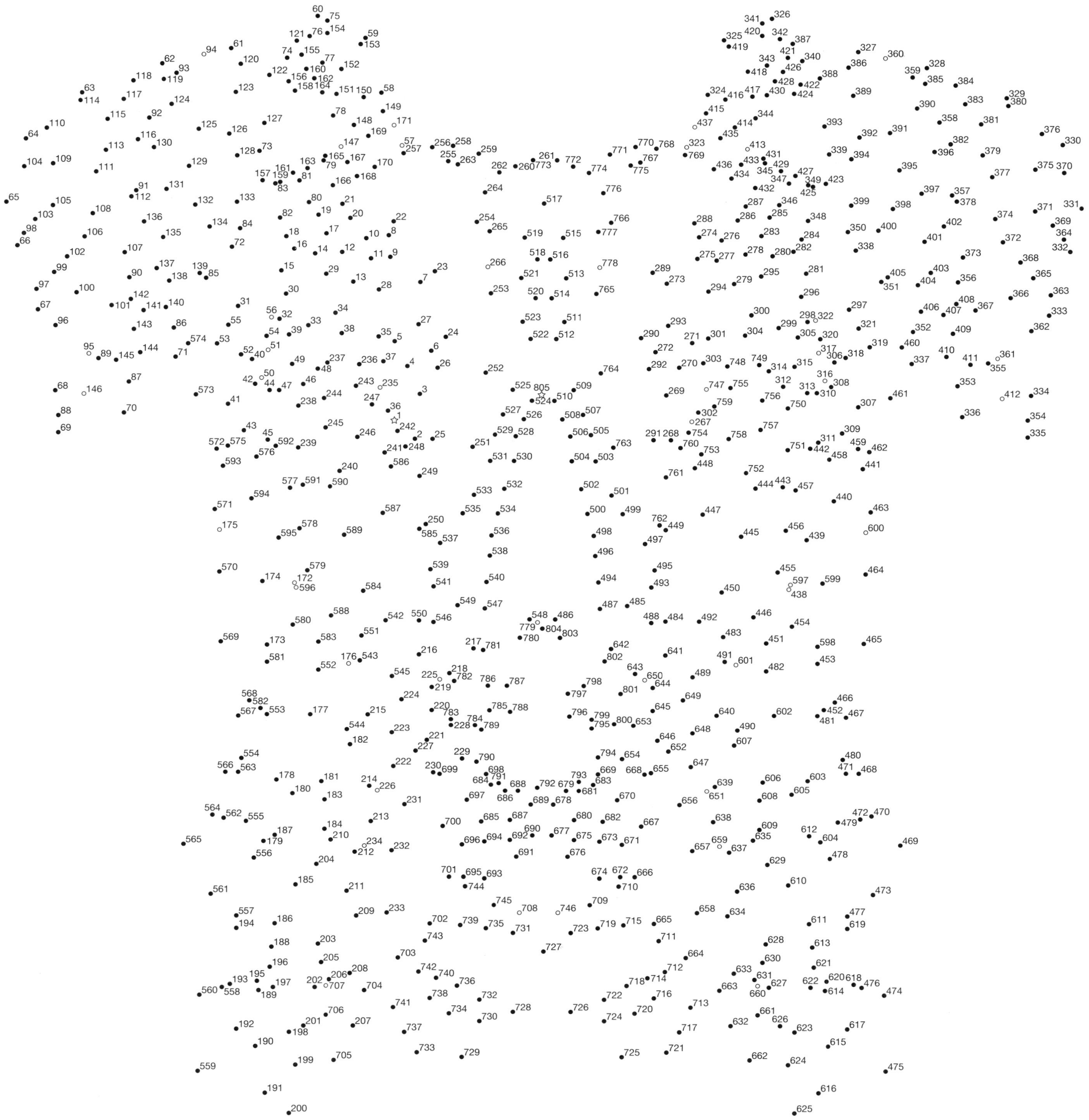

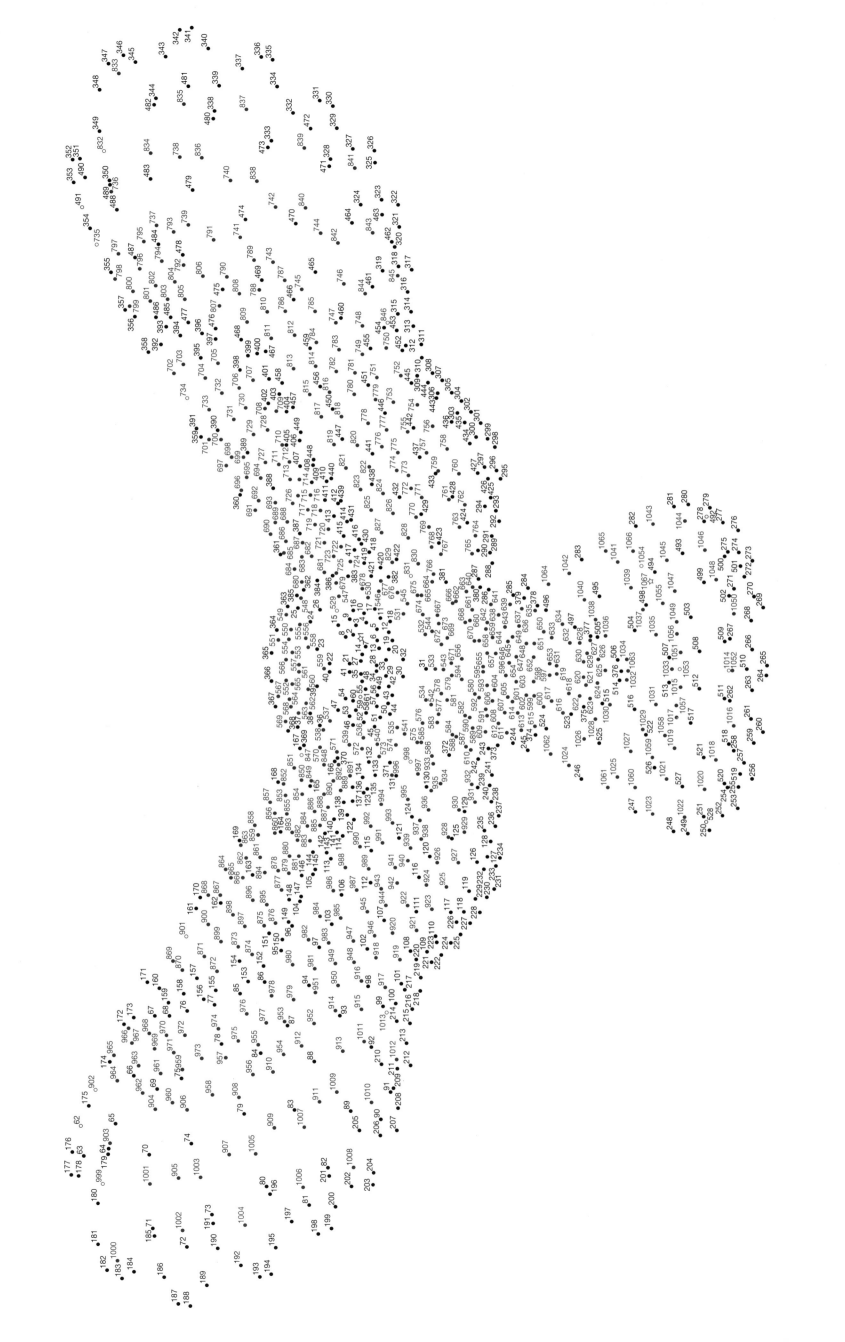

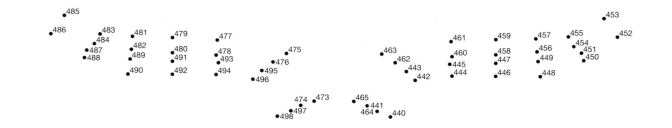

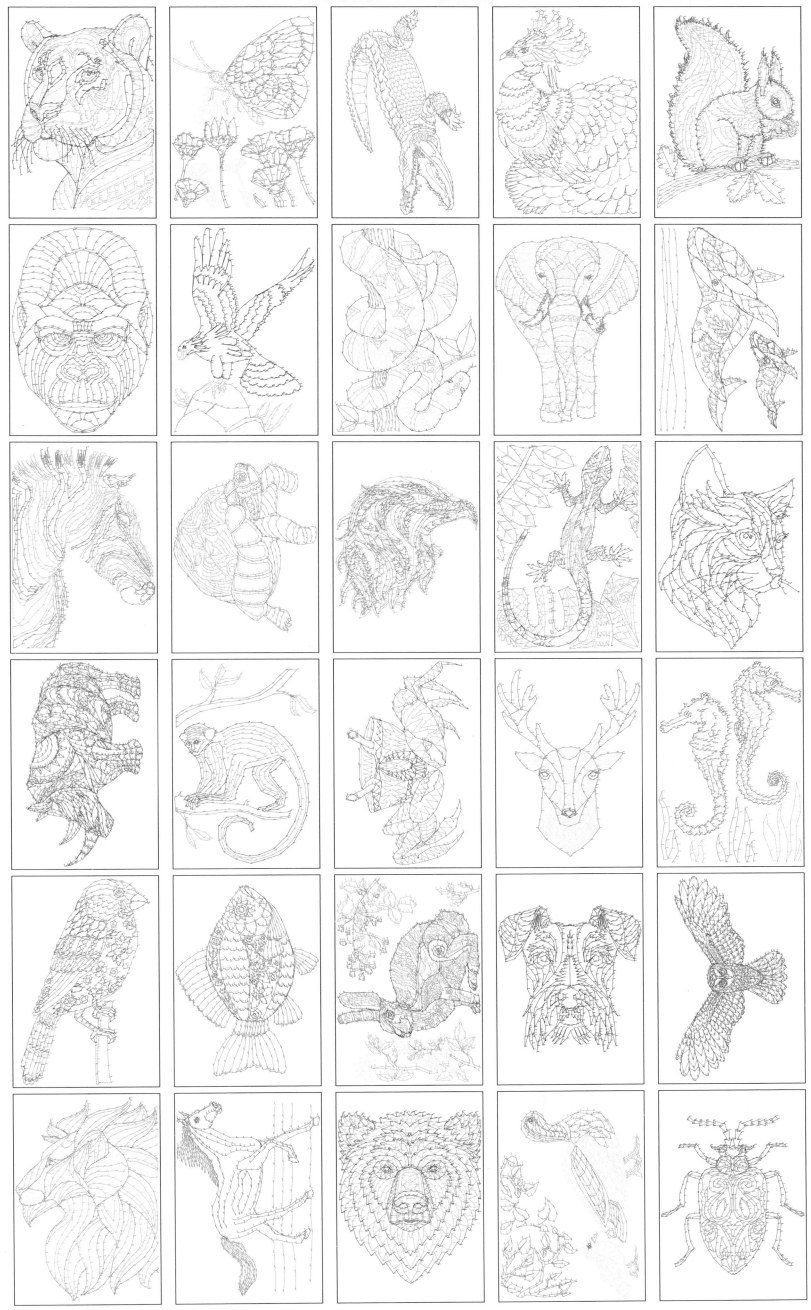